## ABOUT THE AUT

David Mason works in schools all
and abroad, teaching children how to be terribly dramatic and write stories and poems. He has six wonderful children and a lovely wife. They live in Norfolk in a happy, noisy house with an expanding colony of pet mice and two guinea pigs.

## ABOUT THE ILLUSTRATOR

This is the first book with illustrations by Helen Mason, David's wife. The Daleks and the galleon, however, were drawn by son Rory, aged 11.

Take a look at David Mason's website for more information on his work and books and a photo of the family:
www.InspiretoWrite.co.uk

Publishing address: North Street Publishing
1 Millfield Road, North Walsham, Norfolk NR28 0EB
Telephone: 01692 406877 www.InspireToWrite.co.uk
Email: DavidMasonPoet@AOL.com

British Library Cataloguing-in-Publication Data
A catalogue record for this book is available from the British Library
David J. Mason
ISBN 978-0-9558898-8-2


Printed by Orbital Print Services Ltd
Staplehurst Road, Sittingbourne, Kent ME10 2NH
www.orbitalprint.co.uk

TABLE OF CONTENTS

# SNOWMAN

There's no man
Quite like a snowman
Well I think whoa man!
He's made of snow man
One day he'll go man
Just like a snowman
Then there'll be no man

**No ma'am!**

# WHY FACTOR

When I get on television
(And it won't take long)
I'm going to entertain you
It's a brilliant new song

It has fifteen verses
Come on and join the throng
When I get on television
With my brand new song

It's a real knee slapper
A dinger and a dong
You can serve it with your spoons
Or bash it with your gong

I've paid off all the judges
To help make their decision
When they decide on who it is
They want on television

When I get on television
(And it won't take long)
They won't get me off.

# SLUG AND THE SNAIL – A REAL AMERICAN TALE

I love a nice fine strawberry
A-swimmin' in that cream.
Some critter's eaten all our crop
Gone spoilt my strawberry dream.

I ain't no detective
But I can clearly see
A slimy silver glistenin'
Criss-crossin' every leaf.

Slippery Slug's gone broke the law
Sheriff's on the trail
This town's gonna reach ol' Slug
And stick him up in jail.

But Slippery Slug bust out of jail
Crawled silent down the street
He's a real tricky customer
See, he ain't got feet.

Slippery Slug his silver trail
'Cross our cabin floor
C'mon men, get on your horse
Why sure, he can't get far.

We rode all night and half the day
We came to the end of the trail
But sir there ain't a slug in sight
No sir, we found a snail.

# MONEY TALKS

I once said
Something of note
Was it a fiver?
Or a tenner?
My mummy said it
Was of real value
But I never
Heard of the money
Again
And even if it wasn't
Of such great note
I'm still waiting
For my change.

# OSCAR THE BUSKER

Oscar was a busker
He played a bad guitar
Crooned out of tune
Like the perfect loon
So the moon made him a star.

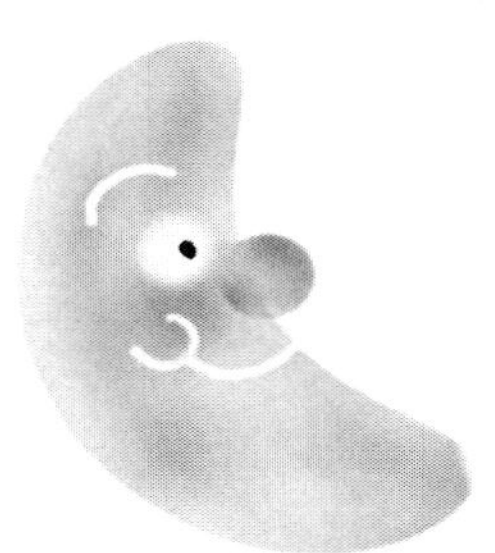

# SPONGES

Children are just like sponges
They soak up all the facts
From the world around them

Don't worry, sponges are just sponges
And don't suck up all the
Children swimming in their sea.

# UPS AND DOWNS

His royal highness, her royal lowness
One of goodness, the other badness
One had dryness, one had dampness
One so mindless, one such madness
One such happiness, one such sadness
One showed prowess, one so careless
One from Totnes, the other Skegness
One so hapless, one so careless
One was godless, one was no less
His royal highness, her royal lowness.

# TALKING CLOCK

On the wall
The clock with the face
Watches
Me
All week long
Working away in
This, my classroom
Come Friday afternoon
He smiles and shakes
My hand with his own
And whispers
Go on, go on home........

The bee
Is the be all
And end all
For
Without the bee
There wouldn't be
Any fruit at all

# THREE WORDS

Ladies and gentlemen
May I say –
A few words.
There, I've said them
And that's

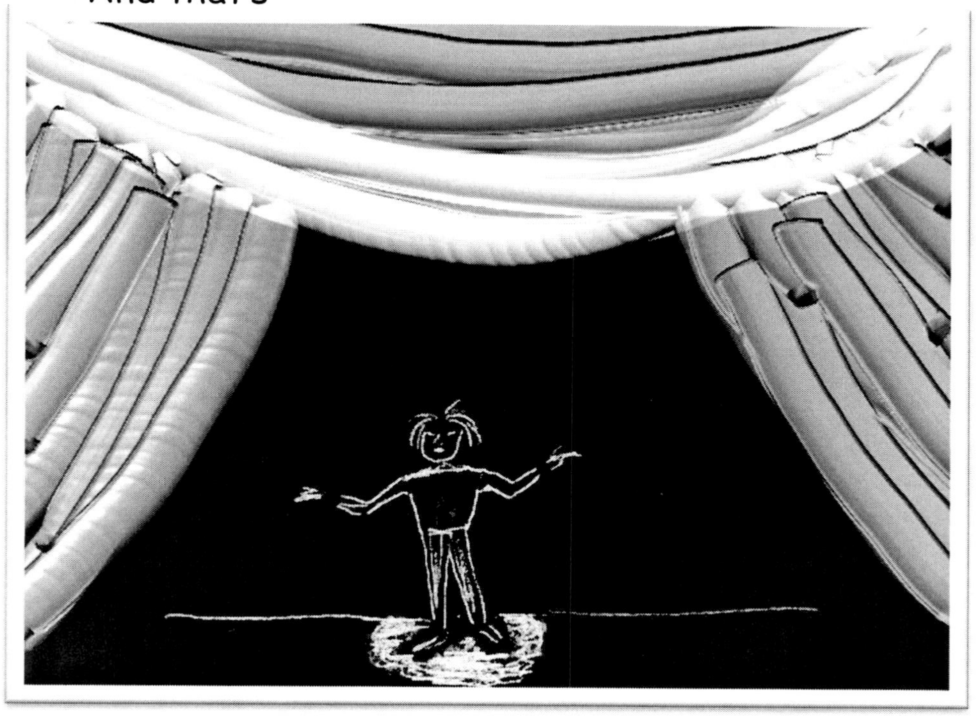

The end of my poem.

# LET GO!

Life is like a ship
That sails the great wide sea
You my friend are captain
You steer your destiny.

Life is like a ship
The stormy swell you'll feel
But all the time you must hold tight
Sure hands upon the wheel.

Yet what if one fine day
You should throw caution to the wind
And find yourself adrift at sea
What then? My hapless friend.

You'll most likely feel better
Relax, a cup of tea
A nibble of ship's biscuit
You float idle on the sea

Where no one can find you
Nothing's ever planned
And there's only the sun
And the sea and the sand

And mermaids, treasures, shipwrecks
New lands to explore
Other lives go sailing by
Who knows what lies in store?

Your beard down to your ankles
Your clothes a rat-tat-tatter
But out here where we've lost control
It doesn't really matter.

Life is like a ship
Hands tight upon the wheel
Or maybe take a well-earned break
Depends on how you feel.

# OPERATION POETRY

I knew an old poet
As deaf as a post
Most of the time
He was poster than most

Oh man, can't you hear me!
I cried in despair
Perhaps you've a poem
Stuck in your ear.

We visited the E.N.T.
The doctor took a look
Ah yes! I've seen this sort before
And read him like a book.

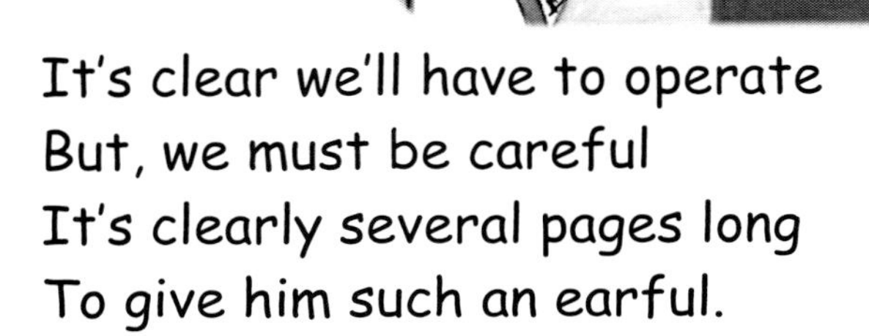

It's clear we'll have to operate
But, we must be careful
It's clearly several pages long
To give him such an earful.

The surgeon, sweat upon his brow
Yet cool, he did not curse,
Inserted in the patient's ear
A sucker for his verse.

Out came all those choruses
The long words and the letters
The poem wasn't up to much
But his hearing was much better.

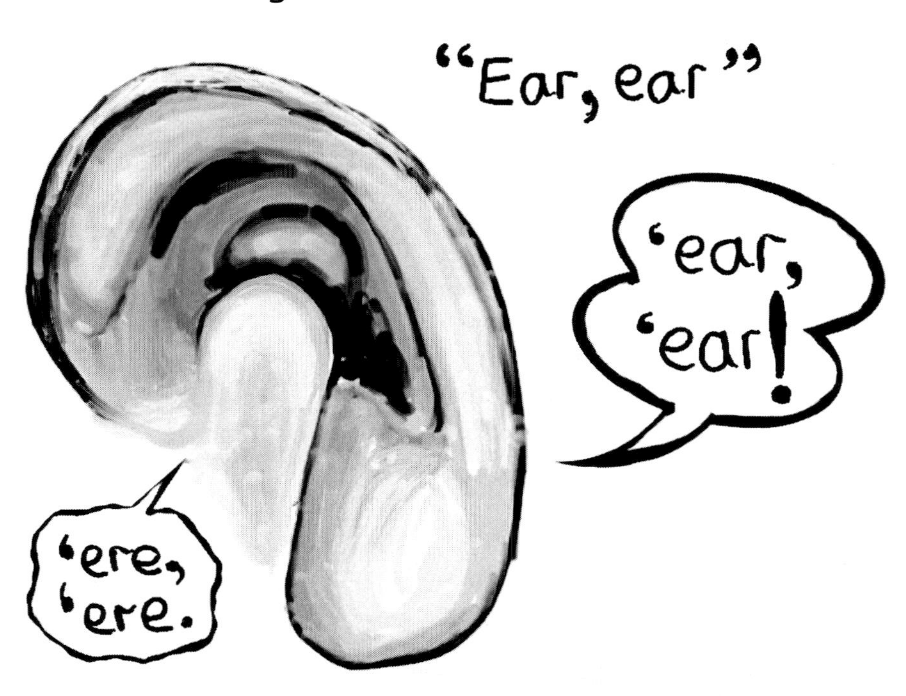

# DEAR QUEEN

My nana is about your age
And she needs a lot of care
So I'm writing to ask you
In secret to surprise her
And also because she likes you
But never learnt to write at school.

Her house is falling down
And when they've got her out
They're going to bulldoze it
She'll be homeless in real trouble
Could you let her live in a castle
One of the ones you're not using?

She doesn't have any real friends
She says they're all dead
Or moved to new houses
I've seen the people following you
She wouldn't need many, just a few
Enough for a cup of tea and a chat.

Don't worry too much about heating
She lives in a place which is freezing
And Nana never ever complains
And don't worry she has her own food
And says she manages very well thank you
Even though I think she's too thin.

P.S. It wouldn't be good to try to meet her
She'd be too excited and fall over
And anyway she's allergic to your Corgis
But I know you can make things better
That's why I've bothered to write this letter
And you are the Queen after all.

# SURPRISES

Life you know
Is full of surprises
Good ones, bad ones
Some in disguises.

Now you make sure
You can recognise
Get you own back
...

# WHEN I GREW UP

When I grew up<br>
I could<br>
Have made<br>
A...<br>
Fortune<br>
Mess<br>
Mistake<br>
Habit of something<br>
Difference Name for myself<br>
Effort

Not me, I made poetry.

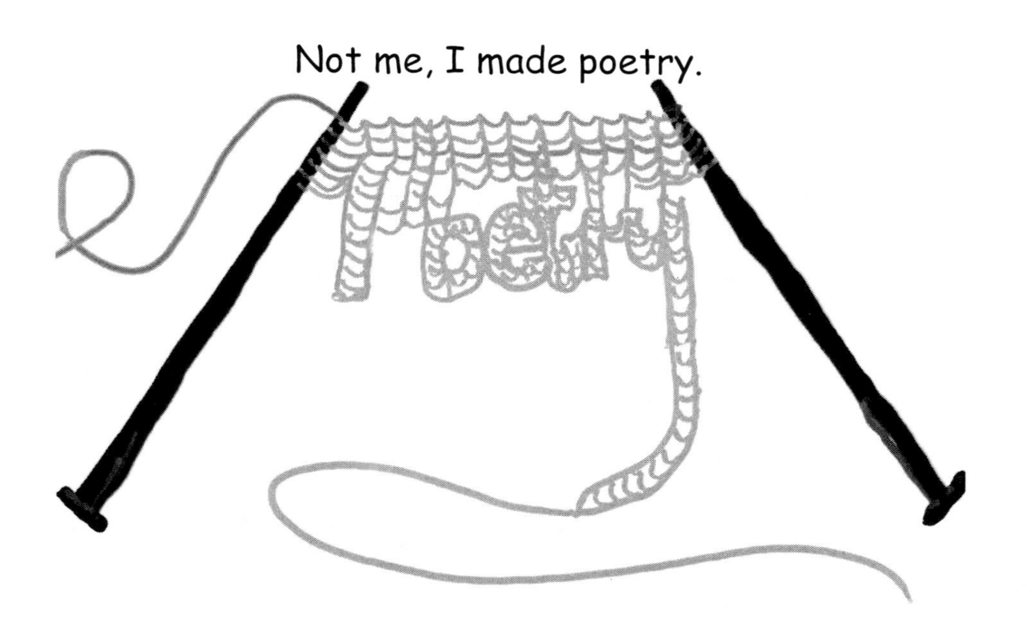

# MONSTER

Hair on the front
The back and the sides
This monster tonight
Has flaming red eyes

Teaches us a lesson
Yet no one can surmise
What it is that's hidden
'Neath this terrible disguise

But back in the class room
You note every feature
Yes! You're being taught
By the Werewolf Teacher.

# MOMENT

I caught the moment
But how about you?
I didn't see it coming
I didn't have a clue.

I caught the moment
But how about you?
I was distracted which
Way did he go?

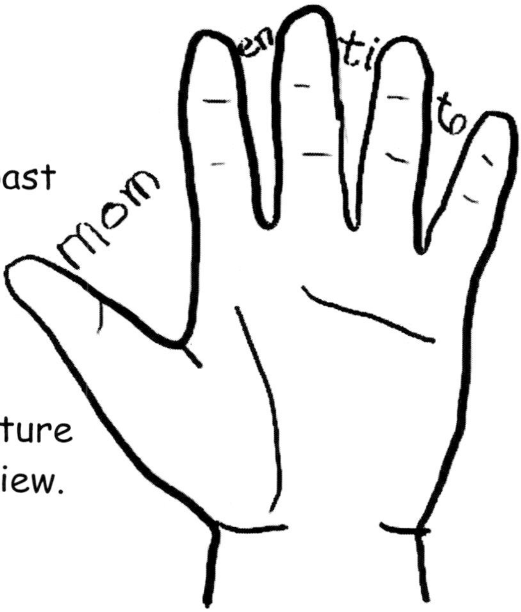

I caught the moment
But how about you?
I was thinking of the past
And how time flew.

I caught the moment
But how about you?
I was looking to the future
He disappeared from view.

I caught the moment
Just as I had planned
But the tiny momentitos
Slipped through my busy hands.

# LIFE WITHOUT CIRCLES

We wouldn't be able
To go round in them.
We would be able
To play rounders or
Ring-a-ring-a-roses
Or find the penalty spot.
We'd have to run
Triangles around people,
Have rectangular arguments
And the earth
Would square up
To the sun.

# THEIR FAULT

How many times
Has my teacher said
It sounds like this but
That's not how it's spelt.

It all went wrong
A long time ago
No one spoke to the
Other and so –

One made the letters
Another said out loud
And we can't do our spellings
When words don't match the sounds.

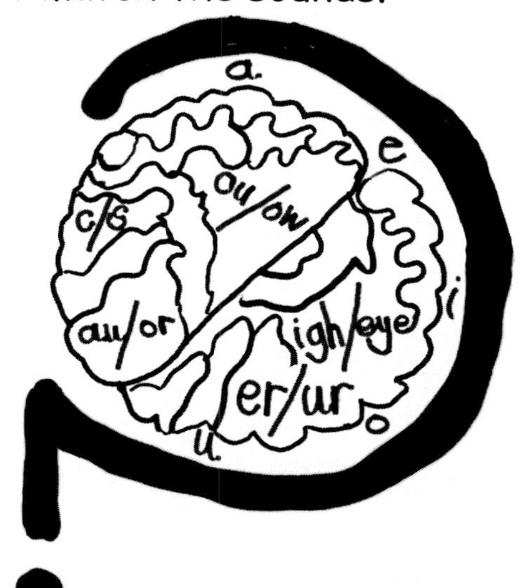

# ALL CHANGE

Spring caught up with Winter
Gave his tail a twist
Summer wore the gloves to cover
Spring's green mitts
Autumn followed Summer and
Hid out in the park
But Winter found Autumn
All alone in the dark.

# CAN'T

I can't tie these laces
I can't tie this tie
I can't find my trouser leg
And I can't see why.

I can't find the fingers
I can't fit the gloves
I can't do these buttons up
I can't find the holes.

I can't find the dresser
I can't find the wardrobe
I can't find my new shoes
I can't find my clean clothes.

I cannot be bothered
I can't get this zip undone
I cannot go out today
I can't – I've nothing on.

# DON'T ASK

We're following the leader
The leader the leader
We're following the leader
Wherever he may go!

We're following the leader
The leader the leader –
But why?
I haven't a clue!

# DEAD DINNER

I look at my school dinner
It stares back at me
It isn't alive
Its eyes are open
But it says nothing
It is not breathing
It does not move
It has no pulse, it is cold
It has suffered enough
I want to bury it
Dinner lady says no
I ask the doctor
He strokes his chin
He shakes his head
Pronounces my school
Dinner dead.

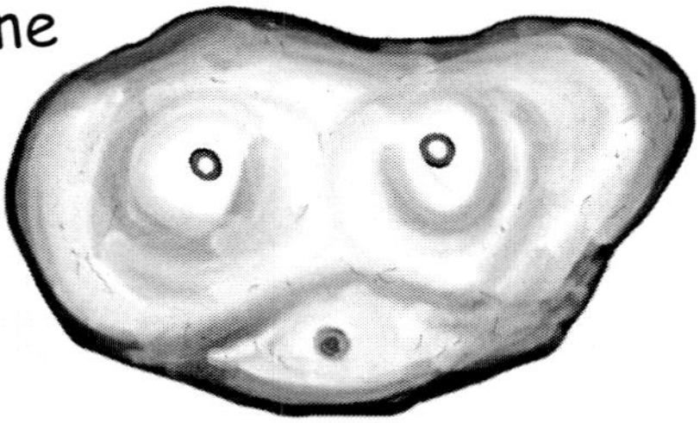

# MUMS AND DADS

Dads need to
Sit down
Switch off
Have a snooze
Say they're busy
Think it over
Later

Ask you why you're
Still not in bed
Tell you it sounds
Far too exciting
Ask you if you have
Any idea how much it costs and
Tell you the answer is definitely
No.

On the other hand
Mums will do
Anything for
A quiet
Life.

# IN CASE OF FIRE

If caught up in a fire
Do not panic scream or shout
Find the nearest fire exit
And let the fire out

And should he insist on smoking
Make sure he does OUTSIDE the building.

# WHEN SMILE WALKED INTO TOWN

It was early in the morning
When Smile walked into town
Folks, they couldn't help themselves
They put their worries down.

This here face is loaded
Says Smile with a grin
You people gotta help yourselves
And learn to smile again.

But Sir, we don't know how to
Says one cute little kid
Ain't no one ever smiled round here
In all the time I lived.

Ah son, you gonna make me sad
But no, I'm Mister Smile!
Now take a good long look at me
Yeah concentrate a while.

Why sure, I feel better
Said the cute kid with a grin
Say Mister I sure feel good
Now I can smile again.

Well, Son, you take that face of yours
That's shining like the sun
You pass that smile on to folks
We've only just begun...

...Why sure the town is happy
Folks stop you on the street
Shake your hand and tell you
Isn't life just great!

Although we have our sadness
We've riches in our life
And best of all, oh yes siree!
We folks have learned to smile.

# THE GOOD LIFE

There is a whisper
A very tiny sound
Going around,
The rustling of the leaves
The gently breeze
Amongst the flowers of the field -
Life is good
Pass it on.

There is talk
Lots of it
The diamond studded sea
Is saying it
And you simply can't silence
The dawn chorus -
Life is good
Pass it on.

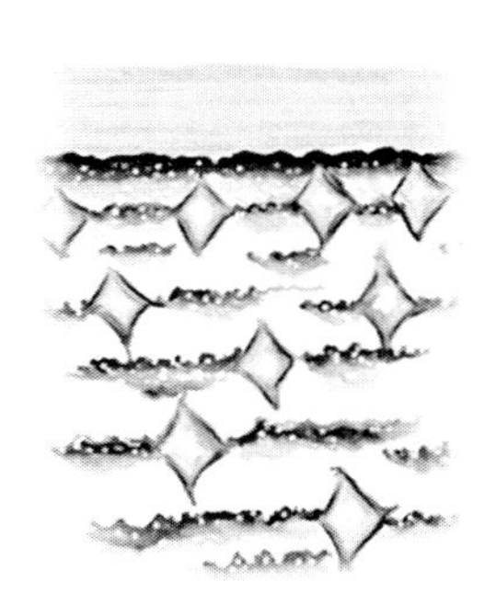

Life is good
So pass it on
Echoes on the mountain's
Lonely tops
Roar of the river's
Foaming froth -

Please one moment
Turn and STOP

Pick up the whisper
See them talking
Feel them shouting
Life is for listening.

Pass it on
Pass it on
Pass it on.
A nod and a wink
So what do you think?
Isnt' life good?

# HIGHLIGHTS

My Mummy's had highlights
Put in her hair
Now when Daddy
Misses the football
He can look at
Her instead.

# CLEAN SHEET

Some football teams
Manage to keep
A clean sheet
Where is it kept?
Do they share it?
Or do some of the players have to
Sleep in dirty bedclothes?

# WOW, MUMMY!

My Mummy says things
Are just indescribable.
I think my Mummy
Needs to go back to school
Where teacher can show her
A list of WOW words
To help her describe
All the nouns in the world
And teacher will give her
Some new verbs too
To show her what
Those nouns can do
And Mummy can learn
To use her connectives
To join up her nouns
And her verbs and adjectives.
Teacher says Mummy
Is top of the class
She's writing such
Beautiful sentences
And I'm so proud
Of my Mummy too
I just can't find the words
To describe her to you.

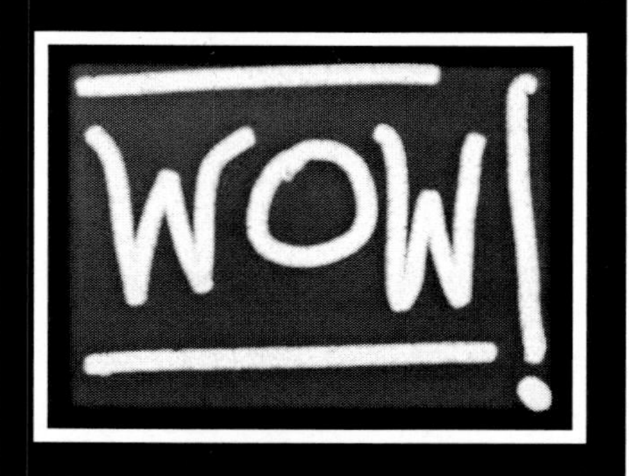

# I'M GLAD

I'm glad I'm not
An adult yet
Adults can't have fun
I'm glad I'm not
The teacher whose
Homework's never done.

I'm glad I'm not
A rich man
With all that cash to count
I'm glad I'm
Not the government who
Say without a doubt.

I'm glad I'm not
The top of class
Yes it's a long way down
I'm glad I'm not
The king whose head
Won't always fit the crown.

I'm glad I'm not
A football, a stump
They use for cricket

Every time I came to
Play they'd take my
Head and kick it.

I'm glad I'm not
The rubbish that lies
Beneath your feet
I'm glad I'm not
The bottom who's
Always underneath.

I'm glad I'm not
A zero a nothing
Counts at all
I'm glad I'm not
The tiny one, the
Smallest of the small.

I'm glad I'm not
Another, a someone
Else, not me
I'm glad I am
The person who I
Was meant to be.

# POTATO

One potato
Two potato
Three potato
Four
Five potato
Six potato
Who are these
Potatoes for?

# STAFF LOSS

In the teachers' lost property
This week we have
    A memory
    A mind
    Some marbles
And
    It.

# WHEN I GROW DOWN

When I grow down
I want to be
More of a seedling
And less of a tree
Or at least
Find the seedling
Inside of me.

# SHORT STORY

They're lined up at the starting grid
Beginning, Middle and End
Oh no, Beginning's ended too soon
And Middle's finished before it started
But the End is nigh
He's just crossed the finishing line!

The End by David Mason.

# MY FIRST (AND LAST) DAY AT SCHOOL

My first day at school was hard for me
I had to stay there from nine until three

But that terrible day has come and passed
And things aren't so bad as it is my last

You see, I've noted one of their rules
The afternoon bell means the END of school

Well I left the building at three PM
And I won't have to go there ever again.

# UNFAIR SHARE

Everyone is sure there's
Enough to go round
But some people are
So busy moving
In circles
That others have
Little or nothing
And for them their
World has stopped turning.

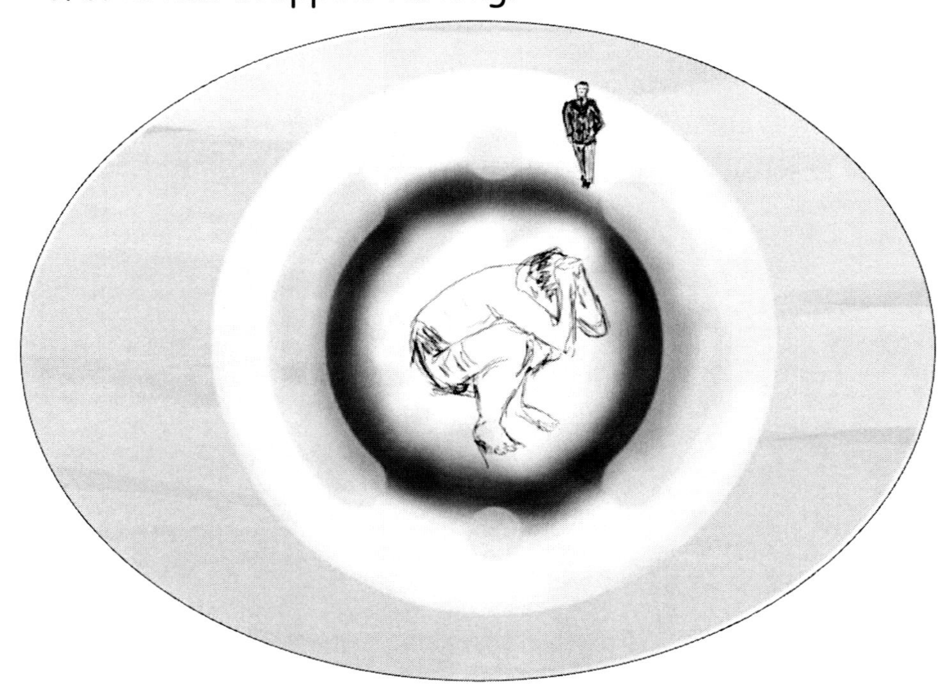

# SKILL

Have you ever seen
A moth playing football
On the street
And dribbling so skilfully
The mothball
At his feet.

# PAY ATTENTION

Hey!  Don't look now!
OK do
Someone's walked into our
Classroom!
Wow!  It's a child with a note
Wow!  It's another teacher
Wow!  It's an alien
Oh no, that's just the headmaster!

Whatever it is
It's a distraction!
It's a distraction!
What's a distraction?
This is, it's fantastic!

Look at the action!
What a distraction!
Hey isn't this fun!

The distraction's only just begun
But when it's over
The only thing left to look at
Is our teacher.

Oooooh
nooooo

# CHRISTMASES

Christmas is coming
The goose is getting fat
The rest of us too
If we don't watch out.

Christmas has come now
Soft whisper, sweet hello
Apologies to one and all
Sorry there's no snow.

Christmas has gone now
The goose is getting thin
Three hundred and sixty-four more days
Before he's fat again.

# PESKY POEM

He's a pesky little poem
A tricky little thing
I think that he's forgotten me
But here he comes again.

He's a pesky little poem
A tricky little thing
I think that I've forgotten him
But here I go again.

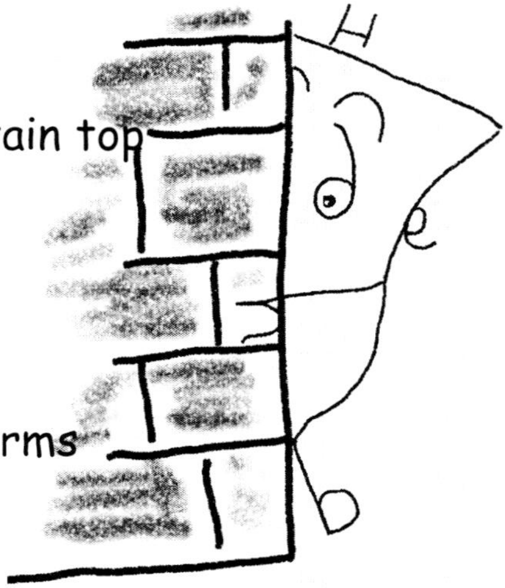

Stalks me in the street
Shadows me all day
I run right up to the mountain top
But I'll never get away.

He prods me in my waking
And tortures me in sleep
Disguis-ed in a thousand forms
He cackles as he creeps.

Just take a look at me, he says
I'm only half a poem
I've slept rough upon your nerves
I need a poem hoem.

And are you not ashamed
Me standing here, half-dressed?
I need a proper make up
And my hair? Well it's a mess!

He's a pesky little poem
A tricky little thing
He says he'll never rest until
I have finished him.

He's a pesky little poem
A tricky little thing
Or at least, I'll say he ***was***
Now take a look at him!
(I've even given him two pages).

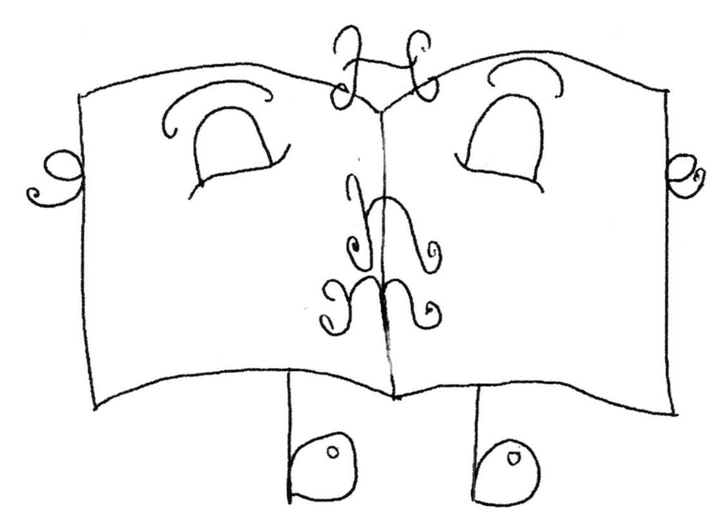

# HOT, CROSS MUM

Hot, cross Mum
Hot, cross Mum
One a penny
Two a penny
Hot, cross Mum
Chasing naughty children
Underneath the sun
One a penny
Two a penny
Hot, cross Mum

# CAPITAL

Every sentence starts with a capital
But I only know of London
That's why every story I write
Ends up being a
Short one.

# ON BEING A HUMAN

What are we to do?
What are we doing
About being human?
Human beings should
Be being not doing
I am a not a human doing
But a human being
We are what we be.

# HOW MANY?

How many grains of sand on the beach?
How many stars in the sky?
How many times have I told you?
Don't ask why.

How many mites in this dusty old room?
How many pigs might fly?
How many times have I wondered
Who put the stars in the sky?

How many tears in the ocean?
How many metres in high?
How deep are the depths we can sink to?
How many times can we lie?

How many answers to questions?
How many times must we try?
How many times must we give up
Before we lay down and die?

Just how close is not quite there?
How much of a near is nigh?
How many times will we miss out?
What size is the biggest sigh?

How many germs on top of a pin?
How many I's in my eye?
How many times have I told you?
Don't ask why.

I feel very scared when
Going to the toilet
Now that I visit
There by myself
The cubicle is dark
And the sides
Of the box
Steep and very high
I wouldn't want to be
Stuck in here I say
But not to worry
I have a VERY loud shout

So I push the bolt, do my thing, pull the bolt and OOPS!
Can someone let me out!

# DON'T TELL ME I HAVEN'T A CLUE

Well it's one for the monkey
Two for the sloth
Three to fetch Neddy
Now go, Rat, go!
But don't you
Tell me I haven't a clue
You can do anything but don't
Tell me I haven't a clue
Clue, clue, I haven't a clue
Clue, clue I haven't a clue
Well you can do anything but don't
Tell me I haven't a clue.

# PET POEM

I have a new pet poem
(I hope he likes this hoem)
I take him
For a walk
Around my head
Every morning.

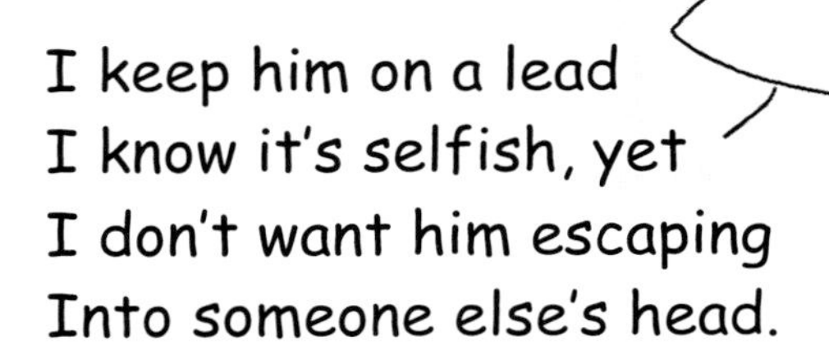

I keep him on a lead
I know it's selfish, yet
I don't want him escaping
Into someone else's head.

I pet him and I fuss him
But let him know who's boss
He wags his verse excitedly
Whilst I stroke his chor-us.

At this moment, he's untitled
But answers to a whistle
So as he is a rhyming poem
I'll have to call him Cecil.

I feed him words and syllables
To make him big and strong
He likes to chew a note or two
I think he'll make a song.

He's definitely a pedigree
He's bred for better things
I think I'll have him published
In all the magazines.

And I won't let him play
With other poems in my head
Who'll teach him all those bad words
And turn him wild instead.

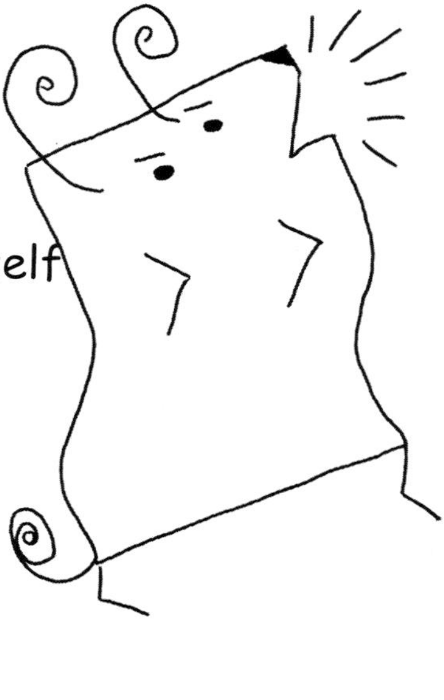

I have nearly tamed him
He's really quite polite
But sometimes he forgets himself
And tells me I can't write.
To which I answer playfully
You know that isn't right
And he admits quite gracefully
His bark's worse than his bite.

# A GAME OF TWO HALVES

Angels at the whistles -

First Half
It was a heavenly day
For football. The sun
Was doing brilliant
Running rings round the earth

Come on you son! Come on you sun!

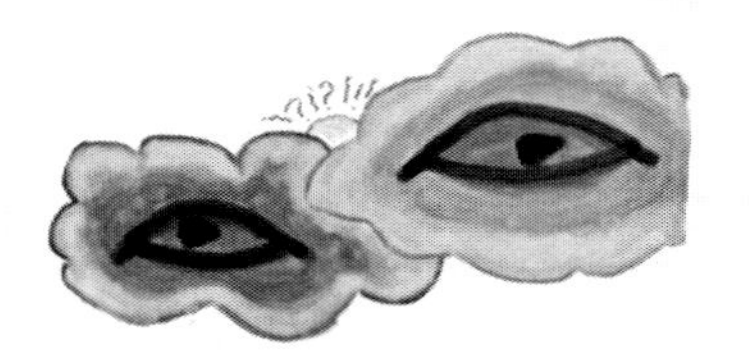

Until the fiendish
Candy floss defenders
Moved in
And smothered him

Get off you clouds! Get off you clouds!

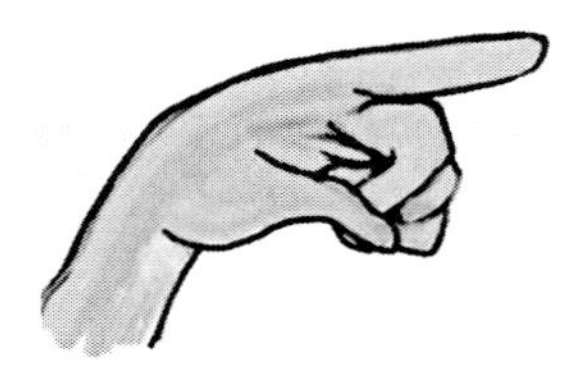

Second Half
But the breeze blew
The clouds a red card
The pitch was pure blue
As the grey disappeared

The opposition were down
To no men
So the sun started scoring
All over again.

# SHOW AND TELL

I show you teddy
You tell me bear.
I show you fun
You tell me fair.

I show you Big
You tell me Ben.
I show you now
You tell me then.

I show you sun
You tell me set.
I show you colour
You show me red.

I show you rose
You tell me hip.
I show you ear
You tell me wig.

I show you teach
You tell me er.
I show you mon
You tell me ster.

I show you class
You tell me room.
I show you sonic
You tell me boom!

I show you po
You tell me em.
Oh no! This is starting
All over again.

# HAPPY SHOP

In the beginning all were sad
Then someone made a discovery
And all about began to grow
The green shoots of recovery:

Hey folks, look here, you won't believe
The happiness we've found
In the shop that sells that happiness
Out on the edge of town.

There were tricks and party jokes galore
There was laughter and merry to make
They were cooking up a feel good feast
With icing on the cake.

There were buckets full of tears of joy
Filled from Heaven above
There was main course for the hungry heart
Pre-packed and ready to serve.

There were tins of liquid sunlight
To chase away the cold
Shelves full of fondest memories
For frail hands to hold.

Freeze-dried fun and tubs of hugs
Fulsome friendly flavour
Jars of pure delight behold
A taste for you to savour.

Carrier bags of woes and cares
Recycled on the spot.
Our motto 'if it makes you glad
We'll sell it in this shop'.

Most folks dance and jigged and played
Smiled the whole day long
They floated up above the clouds
And sang that happy song.

But others couldn't find the store
Out on the edge of town
And when eventually they did
They found it had closed down.

Sorry, sir, we just sold out.
Sir, that is the lot.
Can't sell you no more happiness
Make do with what you got.

So people I am asking you
To share that happiness
There's folks out there in need of it
You know it's for the best.

It's not their fault they didn't buy
Before the store closed down.
Come on you lucky shoppers
It's time to pass it round.

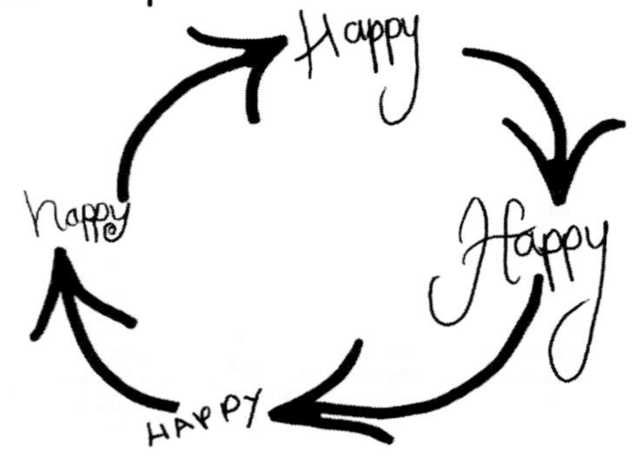

Here comes the rain

drip, drip, drop

Here comes your custard

slop, slip, slop

Here comes the rap man

hip, hop, hop

Here comes the belly

flop, flop, flop

Here comes the jazz man

beep, bop, bop

Here comes the cleaner

mop, mop, mop

Here comes the leaky tap

plip, plop, plop

Here comes the horse

clip, clop, clop

Here comes mosquito

nip, thwack, smash!

# YOUR HONOUR

Are you, David Mason, a writer
Of children's poetry?
I've nothing to say
Your Honour

Did you, David Mason, write
The poem 'Poo on your shoe'?
Indeed, I've
nothing to say
Your Honour

Did you, David Mason, promise
To keep quiet in the future?
I repeat, I have
nothing to say
Your Honour

Wonderful! Then we won't ever hear from you again.

# BRAINY KID

A clever kid
Came into our class
He stood at the front
He wouldn't speak to Miss
Right, he said,
This brain is loaded
Nobody move or
I'll let you have it!

# OUCH!

Mum's pulling her hair out
Dad's racking his brains
I'd rather not do either
It sounds like too much pain.

# AT THE PET SHOP

Buy me! says the puppy
Woof, woof, woof
Buy me! says the birdie
Tweet, tweet, tweet
Buy me! says the kitten
Miaow, miaow, miaow
Buy me! says the hamster
Squeak, squeak, squeak
But the gold fish
Doesn't say a thing
So I know I
Won't be buying him.

# 

It's easy

A peapod is for
Peas
A tripod is for
Tries
An Ipod is for storing
Two or more
Eyes.

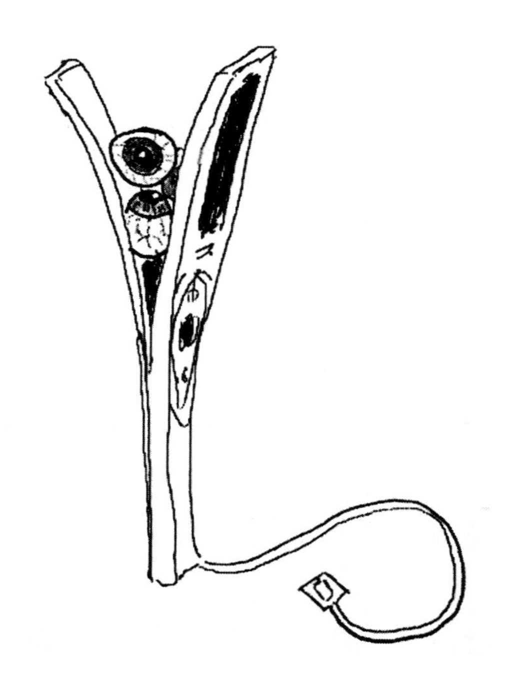

# SUMMER

I love the Summer
What will he bring?
Fish on the fin
And birds on the wing

Sun-starved tourists
To paddle in the sea
A warm one for you
A hotter one for me.

A garden in a forest
Splash of laughter springs
Insects in the undergrowth
Kids crawling on the swing.

Alarm clock children
A day that never ends
Meeting at the park
To unwrap all your friends.

Echo in the classroom
Playground's waiting game
The holidays have come to stay
Each year they do the same.

Yes, I love the Summer
What will he bring?
May be this Summer
I'll bring Summer something.

# SMOKING

I don't like the idea of smoking at all
My friends say it's really grown up
And if I want to be in
The gang I should try it
But smoking doesn't sound the sort
Of thing adults would do

I mean who
In their right mind
Would set fire
To themselves?

# SPRUNG

Ah, that's better
Spring is here
Open up the wardrobe
You'll see the sun appear
Clean out your cupboards
And find the cuckoo there.

The Winter once whispered
The Spring's loud shout
Lift up your floorboards
And let you family out
Put the kids in vases
And watch the new brains sprout.

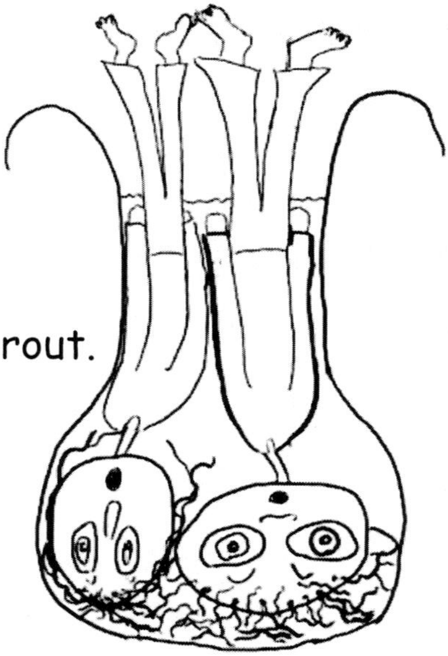

Winter was for resting
Spring is full of zest
Draw back the curtains
The chicks are on the nest
Open up the windows
Spring's out there in his vest.

Winter was a shy one
Spring she wants to meet
Break out of your bedroom
And run off down the street
(But don't forget to bathe first
You'll need a good spring-clean.)

# MUSICAL NOTE

I'm

R of the B
Beast of the beat
Click of the fingers
Tap of the feet

I'm

Mel o' the dy
Hip of the hop
Rock of the roll
Top of the pops

I'm

King of the swing
Queen of the soul
Rhythm of blue
Belle of the ball

When the music stops
I'm

Nothing at all.

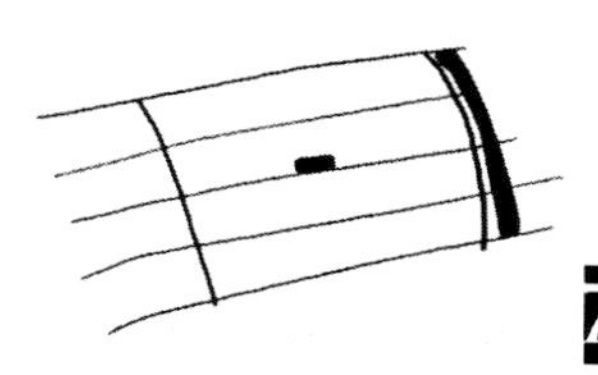

# DALEK PARTY

I went to a Dalek party
Dressed up as Doctor Who
Now, you ask, at Dalek parties
What do Daleks do?

Nothing, really, is the truth
At least not till it's late
Then the party comes alive
As they exterminate, annihilate,
EXTERMINATE, ANNIHILATE,

EXTERMINATE ANNIHILATE,

EXTERMINATE

ANNIHILATE......

# FAT CAT

I drew a picture of a mouse
And another of a cat
Two bits of paper
Just like that
I know my picture of my mouse
And my picture of my cat
Must never get together
Or that will be that
For the cat will chase the mouse
And then where will we be?
The cat's too fat
And there's no mouse left for me.

# MISSING MAGIC MR E

We're getting some breaking news in
Magic Mr E has been stolen!
He was taken last night
From the London Letter Centre
-He was due to perform
His magical tricks there.
Police fear the gang
Will steal the magic from Mr E
And this will change
The way we speak.
Over now, live,
To the scene of the crime...

Sham on you, peopl ar saying
It taks the shin out of everything
The spic out of lif.

It's lik a bad jok
I hop they're happy
Thos terribl swin!

I don't know who is to blam
But things will never be the sam
When all's said and don.

He mad this plac nic
I lov his voic
It mad the world seem fin.

I hat them, I saw
Them driv Mr E down a lan
Through wid gats,
Heaven know his fat.

Polic say, I fear we may los him,
It is a rac against tim
And EEEEEEEEEEEEEE by gum,
We do miss him!

# IF ONLY

If only I owned
All the money
Wouldn't life be
Sweet as honey
If only I was
Crowned the king
I wouldn't have
To work again
If only school
Had not been made
I'd stay at home
And play all day
If only I
Could run away
And not come
Back another day

I
Could teach the class
Hooray for football!
Boo for maths!

I
Could be in charge
You'd be small
And I'd be large

I
Was older too
I could answer
Back to you

I
Could be the sun
I'd chase the clouds
And make them run

I
Could be the day
I'd lock the dark
Night time away

- but
I'd not be me
That would be sad
Don't you agree?

# COUGHIN' ROBIN

He coughed in the classroom
All this term
Sneezin' and a wheezin'
And a spreadin' his germs
All those teachers going out of their heads
Wishin' that Robin was at home in bed

Coughin' Robin – sneeze, sneezy-wheeze
Coughin' Robin – sneeze, sneezy-wheeze
You can tell that Robin's comin'
His yellow nose is runnin', oh yeah

# SLOBBIN' ROBIN

He lolls at his table
All day long
Fumblin' and mumblin'
And gettin' it wrong
He just can't move, he's stuck to his seat
He shuffles his bottom 'stead of usin' his feet

Slobbin' Robin – stuck - on – his – bottom
Slobbin' Robin – stuck - on – his – bottom
Here comes Slobbin' Robin
Never startin' always stoppin', oh yeah!

# WIBBLE WOBBLE

No, I was never much of a dancer, me
I always suffered from two left feet
Until I met this guy with a plan
He said, 'I can really help you, man!'
I have to be honest
I must be frank
If you really want to learn
You'd better start dancin' this dance

*Chorus*
*Wobble wobble wobble wobble wobble wobble wibble*
*Wibble wibble wibble wibble wibble wibble wobble*
*Bibble bobble bibble bobble bibble bobble*
*All night long*

Loosen your neck, let it be free
And shake your head now just like me
Now extend it down your spine
Shake your body just like mine
You have to let it go
Yeah ease that grip
If you really wanna learn
You'd better start shakin' your hips.

*Chorus*
*Wobble wobble wobble wobble wobble wobble wibble*
*Wibble wibble wibble wibble wibble wibble wobble*
*Bibble bobble bibble bobble bibble bobble*
*All night long*

Now move your bottom to the tune
The wibble wobble takes your legs too
Fellas have you seen him move
This boy's body it's in the groove
This place is jumpin'
This boy's king
If you really wanna learn
You'd better start dancin' with him

*Chorus*
*Wobble wobble wobble wobble wobble wobble wibble*
*Wibble wibble wibble wibble wibble wibble wobble*
*Bibble bobble bibble bobble bibble bobble*
*All night long*

Now many years later I'm a millionaire
I wibble and I wobble and I haven't a care
I've moved into a great big mansion
And yeah you got it – I'm still dancin'
Such a success
Take a look, see
If you really want to learn
You'd better keep dancin' with me

*Chorus*
*Wobble wobble wobble wobble wobble wobble wibble*
*Wibble wibble wibble wibble wibble wibble wobble*
*Bibble bobble bibble bobble bibble bobble*
*All night long*

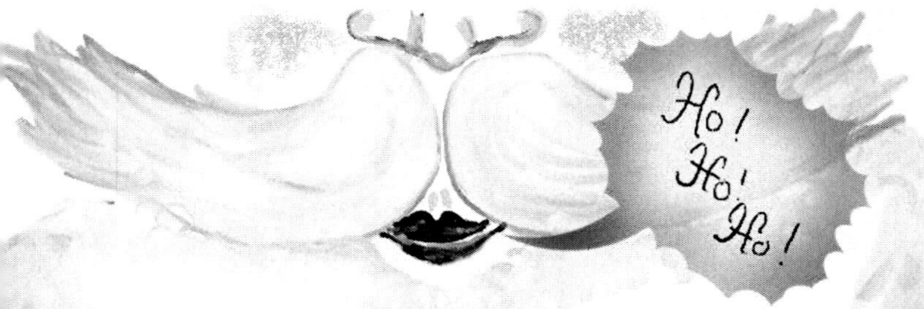


# JOLLY FATHER CHRISTMAS

Jolly Father Christmas
Says a hearty ho-ho-ho!
I'm scared of beards
And I don't get the joke.

# I NEVER EXAGGERATE, ME

I remember one time in the garden
When me mate pushed me out of a tree
I swear it was high as a mountain
But I never exaggerate, me.

I remember one day at the seaside
A tsunami came out of the sea
Lucky that I'm good at surfin'
But I never exaggerate, me.

I remember one day at the sweetshop
They were giving out chocolates for free
I ate so much I was sick on the spot
But I never exaggerate, me.

I remember one day on the footie pitch
This tackle that took off me knee
Still they managed to sew it back on again
But I never exaggerate, me.

I remember one day in the playground
I found this strange looking key
Then I broke into school at the weekend
But I never exaggerate, me.

I remember one day in the classroom
I think it was quarter to three
A monster crept in and took me away
But I never exaggerate, me.

I remember one day I was out in the park
When my friend he was stung by a bee
His head swelled up to six times its size
But I never exaggerate, me.

No I never, ever, ever exaggerate
Not in a billion years, me.

# HUMAN

Fat man thin man
Small man big man

Hi man!  Yo man!
High man low man

Chair man door man
Rich man poor man

Earth man space man
Mad man sane man

Sand man mer man
Her man he man

Start man stop man

Whoa man!

.....Go man!

# GREEDY

Cash in, cash in
Come on get the stash in
Break in, smash in
Grab it while it's going
Cash in, cash in
Gotta get the stash in
Flash her, flash him
Grab it while it's going
Cash in, cash in
Come on get the stash in
Rash her, rash him
Grab it while it's going
Smash it, smash it
Cash it, cash it
Stash it, stash it
Dash it -
Lost it!

# GONE TO THE DOGS

This country, my friend
Has gone to the dogs
Gone to the dogs
Gone to the dogs
Whine all you like
I'm afraid it's the end
We've gone to the dogs
Gone to the dogs.

Collie's in charge of rounding us up
Like sheep we have gone astray
Retriever is fighting to bring back the bite
When Britain once wagged the world's tail.

Jack Russell stroking his whiskery chin
Barks out crime in our cities is rife
Well sniff out this breed, this criminal weed
And lock them in kennels for life.

A four-legged revolution
Alsatian, Dalmatian and all
The Corgis in charge at the palace
We humans have gone to the wall.

This country, my friend
Has gone to the dogs
Gone to the dogs
Gone to the dogs
Grab life by the collar
The bad days are over
This country belongs
To the dogs.

# IT'S CALLED BEING CREATIVE

The teacher told us
To close our eyes
And imagine our way
Into a story

Now try to paint
Pictures with your words

Mine was a long story

With a lot of big pictures
She woke me up
In the afternoon ZZZZZZZZZZzzz
And told me it was
Time to go home.